THE SEA SEARCHERS

THE
SEA SEARCHERS

Men and Machines at the Bottom of the Sea

By TERRY SHANNON
and CHARLES PAYZANT

Illustrated with photographs, drawings and diagrams

GOLDEN GATE JUNIOR BOOKS
SAN CARLOS, CALIFORNIA

FOREWORD

The romance and mystery of the sea have from the beginning of time captured the imagination of man. He has oft gone down to the sea in ships in search of adventure and treasure. However, though the sea has been constantly with man, she has not seen fit in the past to reveal many of her secrets to him. Far less than one-half of this planet has ever been seen or explored, for much of it lies under water. The sea bed with its mountains and valleys, its rivers and canyons, its oil and minerals is waiting the expeditions of seafarers of the deep.

The opportunities to discover and explore the *sea world* belong to you, the reader. The challenge is all around you. The need for oceanographers, biologists, engineers, divers, seamen, and mechanics grows as the nation moves out into deep water.

In order to insure that the great promise of the ocean becomes available to all, in 1966, the Congress of the United States established the Marine Science Council, chaired by Vice President Hubert H. Humphrey, and the Marine Science Commission, its members appointed by the President. Their assignment and goal is to develop and implement a long-range program for the most effective use of the sea.

Terry Shannon and Charles Payzant point up these goals in *The Sea Searchers* as they tell of the vehicles that will open the routes to the sea frontiers. In their excellent work they present the *Nina*, the *Pinta*, and the *Santa Maria* of the present-day "New World" — the world of the sea.

Beverly Hills, California
May, 1968

GEORGE H. SULLIVAN, M.D.
President's Commission on
Marine Science, Engineering
and Resources

PREFACE

Ever since Charles Payzant and I gathered material for our book, *Saucer In The Sea*, which is about the Cousteau Diving Saucer (at that time the only such craft in the world), my desire to go to the bottom of the sea in a submersible had been growing.

Then came an invitation to go down in the submersible *Pisces* whose home port is Vancouver, B. C.'s Deep Cove. On the exciting day of the dive I boarded the power boat *Hudson Explorer* for the trip out to the barge housing the *Pisces*. Until then, in my strong desire to find out for myself "what it's like," I'd pushed the nagging fear of claustrophobia out of my mind. It was just as we drew close to the barge and I saw the *Pisces* in its hangar that the thought showed up, loud and clear, "You are going to be shut up in that little thing with tons of water surrounding you, overtop as well as all around. And you can't get out once you're down in the water — not until the dive is over and you're back at the surface." But there was only a split second of panic; then it left and I felt only keen anticipation for my imminent journey beneath the surface of the sea.

From the deck of the barge I climbed up the side of the *Pisces*, dropped through the 18-inch hatch and on down into the cabin. An electric crane sent the craft out to the end of an overhead beam where we dangled over the water. Mack Thomson, the *Pisces'* pilot, climbed in, closed and secured the hatch. Then we were lowered into the water and down we went. Down, down, and still down to a thousand feet where we rested for a moment on the bottom. We crawled along, stirring up the silt, then rose a few feet off the bottom and crept along through the water, the silt settling behind us.

Alternately stretched out on my stomach or crouched on the tiny pad, I peered through the viewing port at the underwater scene that spread itself before me. Infinitesimal wisps of many shapes, almost transparent but hinting at rainbow colors, formed a continuing ballet as we moved along. These were the elements of plankton which, part animal, part vegetable, are the lowest in the fish-food chain. A jellyfish or two and a bright-hued sea anemone drifted within view. Then, as we groped our way just above the bottom, I became aware of a glittering array of little pink objects shimmering in the *Pisces'* bright lights — tiny shrimp scurrying along, undisturbed by our presence. Then there were patches of coral and a sea cucumber. Never had I been so fascinated. *This was the bottom of the sea!*

I took my eyes from the viewing port for a moment to peer at Mack, about two feet from me, watching from the other viewing port as he guided the little craft along. I took a deep breath. There I was, down the equivalent of a one-hundred-story building, down within the sea under the great crushing pressure of the ocean; but because of the structure of the *Pisces*, the little craft, and we inside, remained uncrushed. I was breathing the same mixture of gases that form surface air, just what I had been breathing at the top when I stepped into the baby submarine. We didn't need it but Mack "bled" in fresh oxygen from the reserve tank to show me how it worked. There was an instant freshening of the air.

Then, eyes glued to the viewing port, I watched the plankton ballet once more as we made our way up to the surface — I couldn't believe that we had been down for over an hour! I had no sense of claustrophobia, only a sense of wonder.

At the top Mack opened the hatch and I stepped out into the familiar world of the surface. But I had been down into the sea, I had crossed the frontier into the new world of inner space — the ancient world of the deep sea. I now knew first-hand what it was like to go to the bottom of the ocean.

Now to those of you who will one day become aquanauts or submersible pilots or oceanographers of one kind or another and help to conquer the world beneath the sea, I can say with conviction, "There's a wonderful world waiting for you down there!"

Corona del Mar, California
May 1968

TERRY SHANNON

ACKNOWLEDGEMENTS

There were many who were most helpful in making this book possible and to them we extend our sincerest appreciation for their wonderful cooperation. Our thanks go to military and civilian personnel attached to the United States Navy's Deep Submergence Systems Project Office, Chevy Chase, Maryland; its Technical Office in San Diego, California; and those at the Naval Underseas Warfare Center, Pasadena, California. Also to Dr. George H. Sullivan serving on the President's Commission on Marine Science, Engineering, and Resources, who so kindly checked the manuscript and wrote the book's Foreword; and to the following companies or organizations:

General Dynamics Corp., Electric Boat Division
General Electric Co., Re-entry Systems
General Motors Corp., AC Electronics
Grumman Aircraft Engineering Corp.
Hydrotech Co.
International Hydrodynamics Co., Ltd.
Lockheed Missiles & Space Co.
Marine Technology Society
North American Aviation, Inc.
Northrop Nortronics
Ocean Systems, Inc.
Ocean Systems Operations, North American Rockwell Corp.
Reynolds Metals Co.
Westinghouse Electric Corp., Underseas Division

Reynolds ALUMINAUT

Reynolds Metals Company

10

The sea is alive today with more things than fish moving around beneath the surface. And so it is that new sagas of the sea are in the making — true tales of adventure, discovery and conquest. They are tales that would fill with amazement the likes of Marco Polo and Columbus, or those who manned the research vessel *Challenger* only a century ago.

The exploits of those men took them *over* the surface of the sea in a quest for trade, treasure, new worlds to conquer, or knowledge of the sea.

Now a new breed of adventurer is plunging deep *beneath* the surface in a quest for knowledge of the sea and to search for treasure. A new breed of explorer is going down into the ocean with plans to conquer and colonize the vast rich underseas world that lies at our very feet. The new breed is pushing back a mighty frontier that has more promise for practical use than does outer space.

The lure of reclaiming one of the thousands of sunken ships that litter the bottom of the ocean has enticed men of daring since the earliest days of sailing. The dream of salvaging lost treasure has been kept alive for centuries. And in more recent years men have come to realize that the sea contains untold treasures quite apart from ships, Spanish doubloons, old wine jugs, or cannon.

Men concerned with ocean science now know that the sea holds an unlimited source of natural treasures. Beneath its surface lie bountiful supplies of food, minerals, and oil that are ours for the taking. *But the taking will not be easy*, for the sea holds challenge as well as promise, the sea is foe as well as friend.

General Motors' DOWB (Deep Ocean Work Boat) is designed for work at depths to 6,500 feet beneath the surface and has an air supply for two men for 65 hours. This nimble craft is intended for anti-submarine surveillance, scientific research, and the placing of instruments on the ocean floor.

The sea is a hostile environment for man, the land-dweller, the lunged-breather-of-air. Yet there are men who look forward to the day when they will no longer belong to the land but will become true dwellers of the sea, complete with artificial gills.

But today's man is not waiting until the day of the gilled fish-man to go exploring beneath the sea or to perform surprising tasks within its depths. Today's man has already set about to find ways to unlock secrets held fast by the sea since time began, to unravel the mysteries that surround ocean currents, giant undersea waves, the habits of fish. He is setting about to discover at first hand what can be read from the layers of ooze and mud at the bottom of the sea, slices of pre-history waiting to be decoded.

Hard-hat diver

Already man is taking steps to put to his own use the natural resources within the great treasure-house of the sea. Conventional tools are of little use underseas. Conventional submarines built for military use are of no value for research and first-hand observation of sea life and vegetation, inspecting underseas cables or surveying potential oil or mining operations.

So today's man while still a land creature is creating new tools, new techniques, new salvage equipment, and new vehicles for use beneath the sea. He is devising ways to stay below and work on the ocean floor, and designing houses in which to live while there.

Already men have designed, built and put to use astonishing machines and equipment to aid in the dramatic invasion of the aquatic world.

Over the years man has penetrated the sea by various means. He has made short dives on sheer lung power. He has made use of hard-hat equipment, tethered to a surface air supply. He has gone down as a free-diver, taking his breathing supply with him in tanks on his back. By these means, the deepest to which he could safely go was about 350 feet.

Scuba-equipped free-diver at work

In a protective shell, such as General Dynamics STAR II, man can take photographic and other equipment to depths far beyond the capabilities of free-divers. Cables can be inspected, geological surveys made.

General Dynamics Corp., Electric Boat Division

Now man has put a pressurized, protective "shell" around himself in which he can safely go down deeper and stay longer than as a wet-diver. This shell is a new-type submarine, a DR/V (Deep Research Vehicle), generally called a submersible. In this kind of plunging into ocean depths people who are not divers can go below to observe the world beneath the sea. They require no decompression since, as in high-flying planes, they breathe "surface air." No special attire is needed and they step out of the submersible as dry as they stepped into it for their journey into the sea.

General Dynamics Corp., Electric Boat I

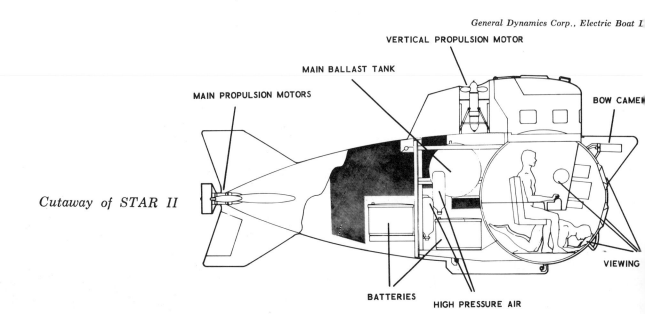

Cutaway of STAR II

VERTICAL PROPULSION MOTOR

MAIN BALLAST TANK

MAIN PROPULSION MOTORS

BOW CAME

BATTERIES

HIGH PRESSURE AIR

VIEWING

Photography Unlimited — Ron Church

Captain Jacques Yves Cousteau, famed French underseas explorer, built the first maneuverable submersible, *La Soucoupe*, (*The Saucer*).* When the Saucer took to the underseas in 1959 it ushered in a new era in oceanographic work and exploration. The revolutionary little vehicle, carrying pilot and observer, can dive, hover, climb, tilt, and turn on its own axis. It is fitted with headlights, cameras, and a mechanical arm which can pick up bottom samples and place them in a catch-pocket for return to the surface. The Saucer can dive to 1,000 feet, slip through narrow canyons, and climb the almost vertical walls of undersea cliffs. It carries a twenty-four hour oxygen supply, but average diving time is four hours.

*See *Saucer In The Sea,* by Terry Shannon, Golden Gate Junior Books, 1965.

Shannon — Payzant

The Cousteau DIVING SAUCER, the first to open up a new world.

*Westinghouse DEEPSTAR 4,000 on an under-
seas mission.*

Today there is a growing fleet of underseas vehicles of varying
capabilities. These are the pioneering work and research boats of
inner space. The versatile subs carry all manner of gear both inside
and out as they take scientists, engineers, or other observers below
on all manner of underseas expeditions.

16

To fully explore and exploit the sea, men and a variety of machines must be able to perform in a wide range of underseas conditions, perform many tasks. They must work in clear water and murky, in depths ranging from surface to the deepest of the continental shelf areas (about 600 feet). Some must be able to go still deeper, over the edges of the continental shelves down thousands of feet into the great mysterious abyss, down to the deepest places of the deep-sea floor.

They must work in areas where currents may reach from surface to bottom, adding considerable difficulty to their performance. They must work in places where great rivers of sand flow through the water in much the way rivers of water flow across the land. Men and machines must work in artificial light which penetrates the darkness only a short distance. And always they must watch for unknown and hidden dangers.

DEEPSTAR 4,000 carries a crew of three — a pilot and two observers.

Westinghouse Electric Corp. Underseas Division

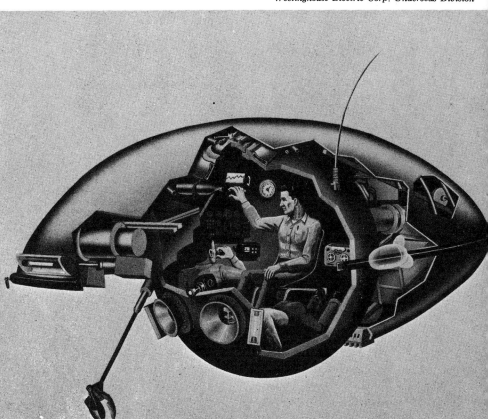

General Dynamics Corp., Electric Boat Division
Much can be learned of the ocean floor from analysis of samples picked up by submersibles such as AUTEC I, built by General Dynamics for the Navy's North Atlantic Test and Evaluation Center. AUTEC's depth range is 6,500 feet.

As they creep along the continental shelves, today's underseas vehicles enable man to pry into the heretofore private lives and habits of sea creatures never before known to exist. They grope through the waters of the Atlantic, scouting bases for underseas research centers. They cut through the Mediterranean, the North Sea and the Red, on archaelogical sorties. They scuttle along in the Pacific, down through dismal waters that lead into submarine canyons that have tantalized marine scientists for years; or in warmer, clearer waters they search out exotic fish. They also work in the deep lakes of the world, making geological surveys, searching for downed planes or performing other missions.

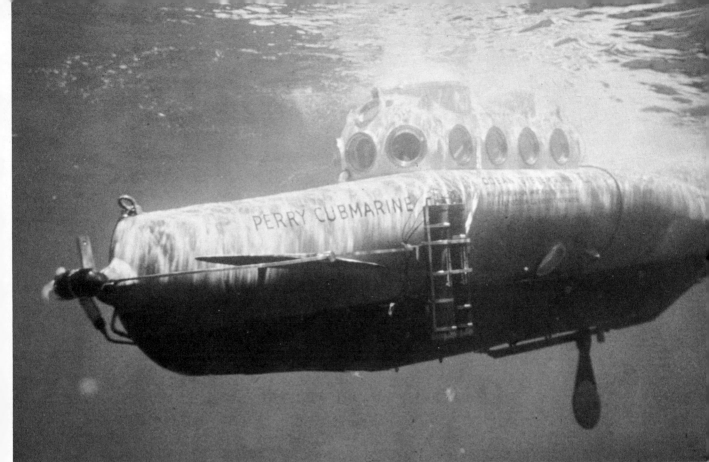

Ocean Systems, Inc.

Perry CUBMARINES, of which there are many, have conducted biological studies for the U. S. Army and Air Force, have harvested black and red coral around Hawaii and inspected trans-Atlantic telephone cables. Here one takes a marine biologist for an undersea study.

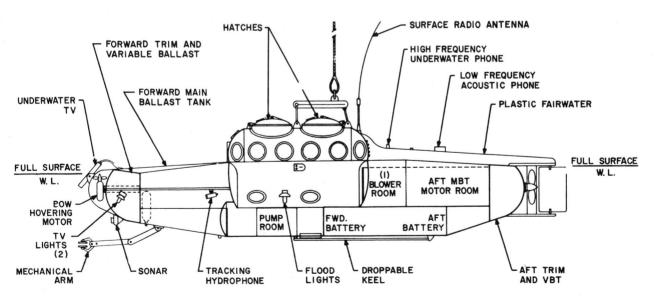

Ocean Systems, Inc.

19

Reynolds ALUMINAUT — thus far the biggest of the submersibles — is the only all-aluminum undersea vehicle. It has retrieved a 198-pound piece of manganese ore from the sea floor, has salvaged current meters from 3,150 feet in the Navy's St. Croix (Virgin Islands) underwater range.

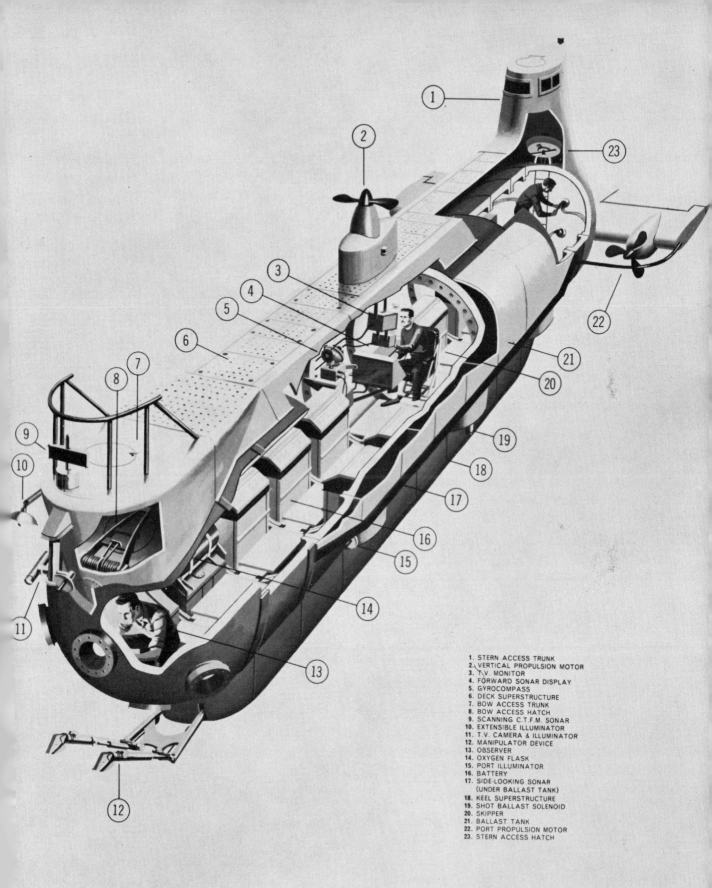

1. STERN ACCESS TRUNK
2. VERTICAL PROPULSION MOTOR
3. T.V. MONITOR
4. FORWARD SONAR DISPLAY
5. GYROCOMPASS
6. DECK SUPERSTRUCTURE
7. BOW ACCESS TRUNK
8. BOW ACCESS HATCH
9. SCANNING C.T.F.M. SONAR
10. EXTENSIBLE ILLUMINATOR
11. T.V. CAMERA & ILLUMINATOR
12. MANIPULATOR DEVICE
13. OBSERVER
14. OXYGEN FLASK
15. PORT ILLUMINATOR
16. BATTERY
17. SIDE-LOOKING SONAR
    (UNDER BALLAST TANK)
18. KEEL SUPERSTRUCTURE
19. SHOT BALLAST SOLENOID
20. SKIPPER
21. BALLAST TANK
22. PORT PROPULSION MOTOR
23. STERN ACCESS HATCH

Reynolds Metals Company

Official United States Navy Photograph

Diver moves clear after assisting with launching of Navy's DEEP JEEP. This two-man steel sphere has a 2,000-foot depth capacity.

Official United States Navy Photograph

DEEP JEEP is launched from General Motors' research vessel Swan.

22

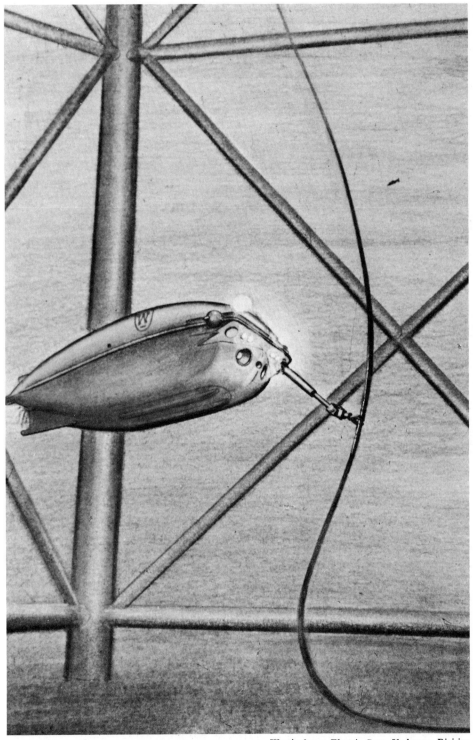

Artist's conception of Westinghouse DEEPSTAR 2,000 working at an undersea installation.

23

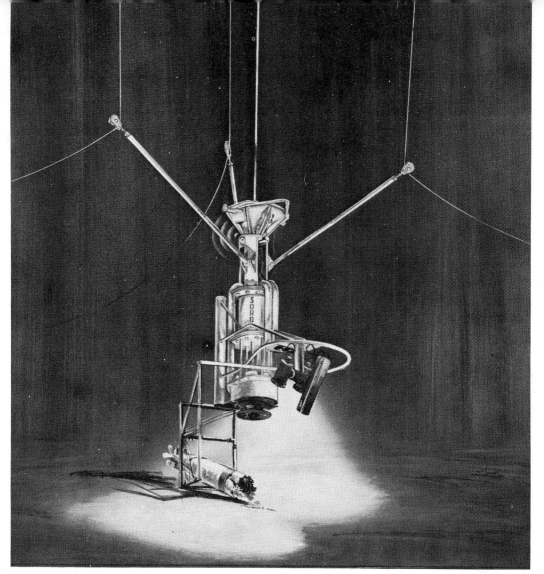

SORD, developed by U. S. Naval Torpedo Station, Keyport, Washington.

Unmanned robot machines, such as the Navy's SORD and CURV, are part of today's underseas work fleet. When marine hardware or other valuable objects are lost in performance of work at sea, SORD and CURV may be used in search and recovery operations. Skilled technicians working on the surface operate the devices, quite different from each other in design and use.

SORD (Submerged Object Recovery Device) sees by TV, hears by sonar, and senses by magnetism. Down where no daylight ever penetrates it can locate an object buried in mud beneath the water, remove the mud, grasp or snare the object, and bring it to the surface. It has brought up dozens of items valued at hundreds of thousands of dollars from depths to 3,030 feet at locations extending from Western Canada to the Virgin Islands.

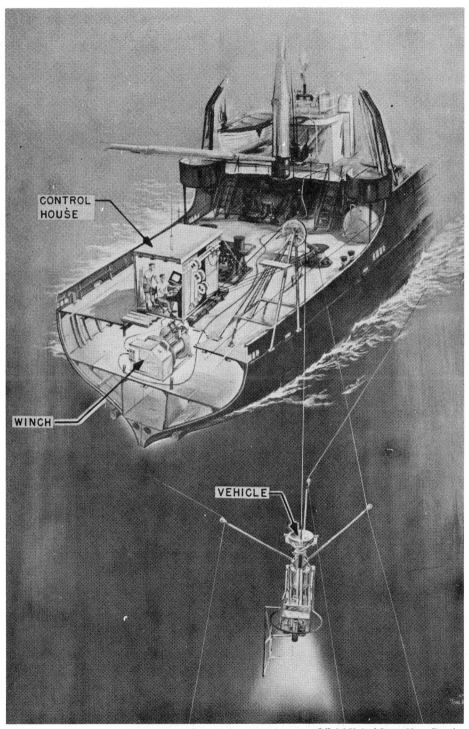

CONTROL HOUSE

WINCH

VEHICLE

Official United States Navy Drawing

Typical installation of SORD.

25

Topside technicians control CURV's underseas activities. This remarkable machine was developed at the Navy's Pasadena-based Underseas Warfare Center (formerly Naval Ordnance Test Station).

CURV (Cable-Controlled Underwater Research Vehicle) also has TV eyes and sonar ears. It does survey work as well as recovery. It can easily inspect the condition of underwater facilities and be run day or night.

CURV

Official United States Navy Photograph

CURV grasps a torpedo embedded in sand on the sea floor.

With its strong lights and a 500-frame capacity camera, CURV has crawled along the sea bottom taking pictures used in mapping sites for underseas habitats. It is designed to work at depths to 2,000 feet, although on one memorable occasion, as we shall see on following pages, it went much deeper.

Official United States Navy Photograph

Sometimes CURV's camera catches familiar objects which have been detected by sonar.

27

In January of 1966 an event occurred that set in motion an underseas search more hair-raising and spine-tingling than any a mystery writer could have imagined. It was the search for a hydrogen bomb lost in waters of the Mediterranean Sea off the coast of Palomares, Spain.

It was vital that the bomb be recovered for security reasons as well as to remove an object of potential danger. It was a hunt in the best cloak and dagger tradition, with alien ships standing by ready to take over the search for their own purposes should the United States fail in its attempt to find the bomb. Coastal villagers were terrified, ready to leave forever their tiny farms and fishing grounds. Their fears had to be relieved.

Men and equipment capable of underseas work were summoned to join *Operation Broken Arrow*, as the bomb search was labeled. Industry as well as naval units answered the challenging call sent out by Rear Admiral William S. Guest (USN), Task Force Commander in charge of the sea search.

Submersibles and other equipment that could be flown to the site were hurtled across the Atlantic in fast-flying jets. *Aquanauts*,* submersible pilots, technicians, engineers and experts in many fields were rushed to the scene. It was a terrible time of testing for men and machines beneath the sea.

The water was alive with hard-hat and free-divers searching a 125-square-mile area of the Mediterranean. Experts such as Jon Lindbergh went to depths unsafe for ordinary divers. Gullies, canyons and steep slopes, as well as more rolling areas, made up the underseas terrain. Looking for the bomb was akin to looking for a needle in a whole wheatfield, let alone a haystack — and that in the pitch blackness of night.

Deep Jeep crawled along the bottom at 2,000 feet. A *Perry Cubmarine* hunted in shallower waters. The little *Alvin* and the big *Aluminaut* went deeper. Tension mounted as the agonizing search went on day after long disappointing day.

---

*Specially trained divers skilled in underseas work.

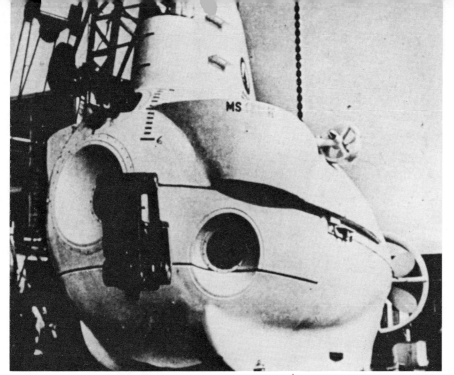

Official United States Navy Photograph

ALVIN

Reynolds Metals Company

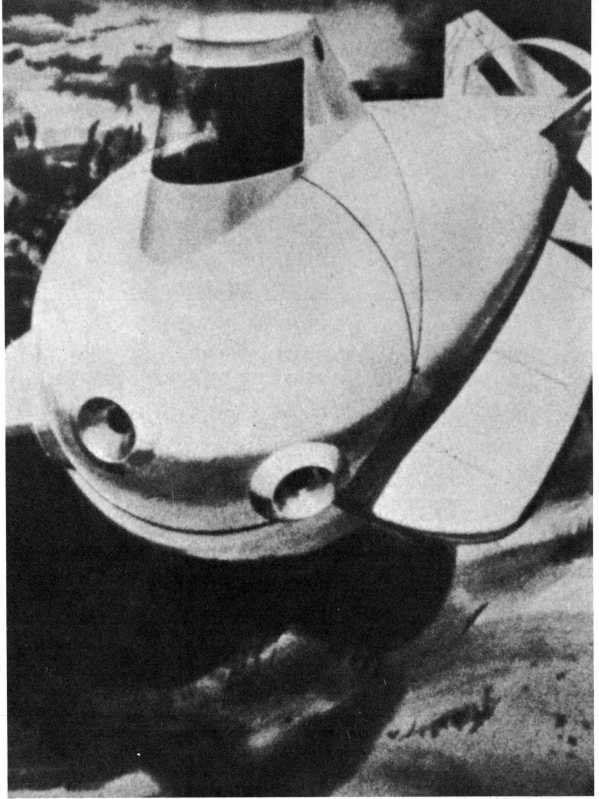

ALVIN, operated by Woods Hole Oceanographic Institution for the Navy, searches for the lost bomb. ALVIN's pilots, William O. Rainnie (chief), Valentine P. Wilson and Marvin J. McCamis, worked in teams of two during the bomb search.

30

Then on March 15 *Alvin* located the bomb! Shrouded in its parachute, it lay in ooze far down a treacherous slope. It could scarcely have been in a worse position. The bomb was too heavy for the tiny *Alvin* and its mechanical claw to lift. A naval research ship, the *Mizar*, pinpointed the bomb's position with special navigational equipment and guided the *Aluminaut* to the general vicinity of *Alvin* and the bomb. Then pilots of the two submersibles, using voice communication, accomplished the first rendezvous of submarines at a depth of 2,500 feet. They met within less than 50 feet of each other. Grappling arms of the *Aluminaut* were not strong enough to lift the bomb, but it stood by, marking the location.

Recovery posed tremendous problems and perils. With its claw, *Alvin* drew the parachute as clear of the bomb as possible, laying it out along the ocean floor as far as it could.

The little sub then fastened lines to a steel work table, lowered for the purpose, and firmly entangled grappling hooks into the shroud lines of the parachute. But cables broke as the table, parachute and the bomb were being raised and the bomb tumbled still farther down the slope.

Official United States Navy Photograph

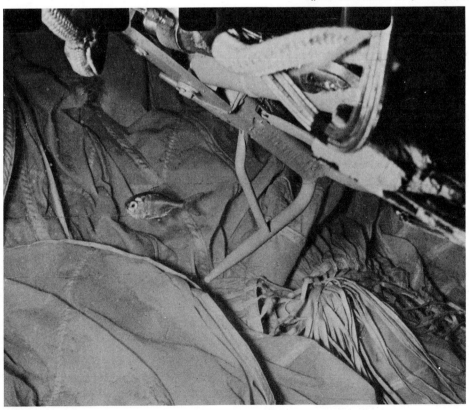

CURV

The frustrating search began again. It was on April 2 that *Alvin's* pilots located the bomb the second time, now at 2,800 feet, and again covered by the parachute. CURV, on the scene now after being modified for this specialized task, was sent down. A line from it was hooked into the parachute and given a sharp yank in hopes of pulling the parachute away from the bomb. This stirred up bottom silt into a great cloud.

With grappling hooks firmly engaged, rise to surface is begun. CURV's TV cameras flashed picture to control ship.

32

Official United States Navy Diagram

The 20-foot visibility now reduced to zero, *Alvin* moved cautiously ahead. Suddenly the parachute was there, directly in front of the craft, billowing out like a circus tent. *Alvin* became tangled in the shroud but the pilots managed to work free and back the sub away before becoming hopelessly enmeshed.

At long last the bomb was hooked securely to CURV and the slow ascent to the surface started.

Anxiety prevails as divers prepare to attach cradle to recovered bomb.

At last! Bomb rests safely aboard ship.

Mission at Palomares accomplished. A tired but elated group of men who worked with CURV stand in front of recovery vehicle aboard USS Petrel.

When the bomb was safely aboard the *USS Petrel*, members of the search and recovery crew were jubilant but too exhausted for any immediate celebration.

The whole world breathed a sigh of relief when the news was flashed abroad that the bomb had been safely lifted from the sea. The people of Spain, particularly those of the Palomares area, gave special thanks as they celebrated the removal of *La Bomba* from their shores. Fear was gone, little farms and fishing grounds were safe once more.

El Alcázar

Madrid, sábado 9 abril 1966. 2 ptas.

Con este número recibirá el suplemento gratuito.

ULTIMOS DIAS DEL CONCURSO

(Bases, en la página 14)

III Concurso de EL ALCAZAR
Europa en sus manos
CUPON

(CORTAR POR AQUI)

¡HE AQUI LA BOMBA!

La bomba perdida fue mostrada a la Prensa mundial a bordo del buque "Petrel". (Foto Víctor Manuel.)

Hoy entra en vigor la NUEVA LEY DE PRENSA

Un documento histórico

Así fue recuperado el artefacto de Palomares

Todas las fotos

Reportaje de nuestros enviados

Official United States Navy Photographs

ASI YACIA EN EL FONDO DEL MAR

Esta es la primera fotografía obtenida de la bomba. El "Alvin", que la descubrió, pudo captarla con sus cámaras fotográficas. El artefacto estaba, en el momento de su localización, como puede apreciarse, cubierto por el paracaídas con el que cayó al agua.

A las siete de la mañana el contraalmirante Guest dio la orden de izar, a bordo del "Petrel", la bomba. Cubierta con el paracaídas, llegó a cubierta, e inmediatamente después fue inspeccionada por un técnico. El general Wilson y el contraalmirante Guest pudieron contemplarla, al fin.

Estas páginas resumen los ochenta días de trabajos intensos, que han sido necesarios para dar fin a la operación "Flecha Rota". Miles de hombres han vivido por tierra y mar la aventura de la recuperación de los cuatro artefactos caídos en España el 17 de enero. Con el hallazgo y rescate de la cuarta bomba la tranquilidad ha vuelto a un pueblo ya famoso en el mundo: Palomares.

FRANCE

FUERZA OPERACIONAL 65

"PETREL"

MAR MEDITERRANEO

ESPAÑA
Palomares

PORTUGAL

2500 PIES PROFUNDIDAD

CURV

BOMBA

Este es el sumergible "Curv", dirigido a distancia, dotado de articulaciones especiales, capaz de bajar, después de las modificaciones a que fue sometido, a 7.800 pies de profundidad.

La Prensa mundial dio cita en Palomar

Más de cien periodistas, españoles y extranjeros pertenecientes a los diversos medios informativos, acudieron al muelle de Garrucha para ser trasladados en barcazas al "Albany". Desde la misma cubierta en que ondeaba su insignia, los micrófonos, las cámaras y los tomavistas captaron el emocionante momento del encuentro con el ingenio nuclear.

De nuestros enviados especiales en Palomar

Textos: JULIAN CANDAU

Fotografías: VICTOR MANUEL y Official Photograph U. S. Navy

Official United States Navy Photograph

Spanish magazines and newspapers, as well as those throughout the world, gave graphic accounts of the events that took place during the "Case of the Missing Bomb."

Combined search operations were a masterpiece of cooperation between those working on the surface and those working under perilous conditions below. Divers had performed heroically. The usefulness of submersibles and other newly developed underseas equipment operated by skilled men had been demonstrated beyond a doubt. Men and machines had come through the terrible time of testing with flying colors.

37

International Hydrodynamics Co., Ltd.

PISCES

After Cousteau's baby submarine amazed the world with its prowess, the big thrust in submersible building was mostly American, mostly by large, well-funded private industries. But other countries are becoming submersible-minded (Japan, Russia, England have made a start), though not all are built by big industry.

Canada's first submersible, the *Pisces*, was built by three enterprising young men. Deep-sea divers all, two worked at their occupation to pay the bills while the third supervised and worked on construction of the vehicle. A self-taught engineer, the craft was built to his design and he became its only pilot.

So successful is *Pisces*' performance that it, like other DR/V's, is in constant demand. England has asked for it. Russia wanted to buy it. Our Navy has used it to search out torpedoes lost in sea ranges during target practice. The Bureau of Commercial Fish-

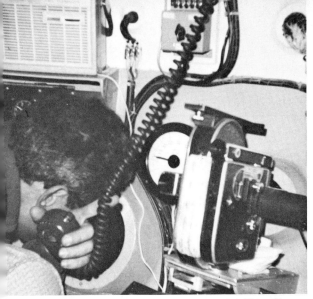

In the cramped quarters aboard the PISCES, Mack Thomson, the pilot, talks to his surface support ship.

Terry Shannon

eries has used it for observing the behavior of fish and to make surveys of the operation of fishing gear.

By early 1968, just a year after *Pisces'* launching, the need for additional craft was obvious. Four more *Pisces* will have hit the deep sea by late 1968 or early '69. One will go to England as the *Vickers-Pisces*, the others will join *Pisces I* to become *Pisces II*, *III* and *IV*. Missions already scheduled for each will take the DR/V's from home port to work in the Arctic on a joint Canadian-U.S. Government project, in California, in Hawaii, and in Canada itself, as well as Washington's Puget Sound.

Piloting a submersible is a highly specialized operation. Danger lurks beneath the sea and safe return to the surface depends upon the skillful handling of the craft by the pilot. In 1966 there were only 15 members in the exclusive group qualified to pilot these underseas craft. By 1967 there were 30, and the ranks are swelling as more DR/V's are built and men trained to operate them.

Mack Thomson

Author Terry Shannon, one of the very few women ever to go down in a submersible, peers through a viewing port during a 1,000-foot dive.

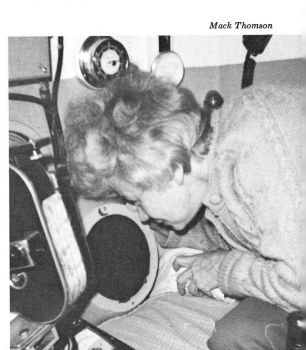

Lockheed Missiles and Space Company

Lockheed Missiles and Space Co.'s research submarine DEEP QUEST has life support for four occupants for 48 hours.

Early in 1968 the four-man *Deep Quest* reached a record depth for submersibles when it touched down on the bottom of the Pacific at 8,310 feet. An inch-thick steel inner hull protects its crew from the crushing pressures of great depths. Its shark-shaped aluminum outer hull is free-flooding, thus water pressure inside and outside the outer hull is equalized. Carried to diving locations aboard its support ship, *TransQuest*, the sub can carry on undersea operations for 24 hours, maintain its crew for 48.

Pilot Glenn Minard (left) and Larry Shumaker, chief pilot, display Stars and Stripes
above banner signifying "Lockheed's DEEP
QUEST was here." Flags were planted 8,310
feet down on the bottom of the Pacific.

Lockheed Missiles and Space Company

Prior to the record dive, a diver completes inspection of DEEP QUEST.

Lockheed Missiles and Space Company

A Lockheed hydrodynamics research
specialist tests a 1/12th scale model
of DEEP QUEST below the surface.

*Cranes gingerly lower the 40-foot DEEP QUEST into tank
for final tests. An important feature is a man-in-sea module.
Divers exit to work on sea floor and re-enter through hatch
in module floor. Pressure inside module equals that of surrounding sea, thus keeping water out when hatch is open.*

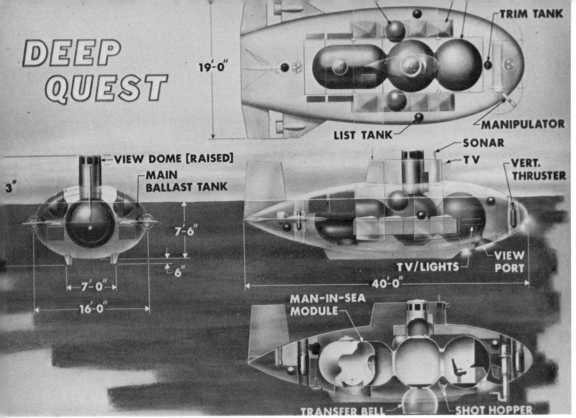

DEEP QUEST

19'-0"

TRIM TANK

LIST TANK

MANIPULATOR

SONAR

TV

VERT. THRUSTER

VIEW DOME [RAISED]

MAIN BALLAST TANK

3"

7'-6"

6"

7'-0"

16'-0"

TV/LIGHTS

VIEW PORT

40'-0"

MAN-IN-SEA MODULE

TRANSFER BELL

SHOT HOPPER

Lockheed Missiles and Space Company

Deep Quest, designed for scientific research and military work, will help in charting the vast part of our planet (nearly three-fourths of it) that lies under water in inner space.

Lockheed Missiles and Space Company

DEEP JEEP's lights try to pierce the underwater darkness.

Oceanographers tell us that the bottom of the sea is no better mapped than the North American continent before the Lewis and Clark expedition. But they know that the underseas world has mountain ranges, deep valleys, and broad plains. There are vast canyons that would dwarf the Grand Canyon and mountain peaks higher than Mt. Everest. Finding the way in this forbidding and unfamiliar world is a more treacherous task than trying to find the way through thick, black fog on the surface.

While some men and machines are busy with mapping expeditions, others are busy with other aspects of the sea. They investigate its geology, biology, and its chemical make-up. Man's quest for first-hand knowledge of the underseas world makes of the submersibles a scientist's dream come true. More can be accomplished in an hour's time in a DR/V than in weeks of wet-diving.

Artist's conception of ALUMINAUT implanting scientific research instrument package on sea floor.

Reynolds Metals Company

Ocean Systems Operations, North American Rockwell Corp.

North American Rockwell's SWIMMER SLED carries scuba-equipped pilot and passenger at speeds up to 2.5 knots.

But the wet-diver can now go zooming through the water in a new entry into the field of underseas vehicles, an open craft that saves valuable time and energy. The two-man craft permits speedy performance of tasks at depths to 150 feet and ranging from sea wall inspection to search and rescue missions, motion picture or TV work — documentaries or sheer entertainment films.

The working submersibles all—big boats, little boats, the deepest of deep-sea diving boats, and those built for shallower waters — are kept on the go. They work under contract for the Navy, commercial firms, or scientists with special interests.

46

Hydrotech Co.'s tiny "family submersible" SUBMARAY can be easily towed from place to place by automobile. It has appeared in TV's "McHale's Navy," taken part in underwater timber surveys and searches for sunken boats and planes.

Hydrotech Co.

General Dynamics Corp., Electric Boat Division

The two-man research sub ASHERAH was built by General Dynamics for the University of Pennsylvania Museum, principally for archaeological research. Equipped with stereo cameras, ASHERAH photographed the 1,500-year-old wreck of a Byzantine galley in the Aegean Sea in one hour. Without ASHERAH, the work would have taken divers several months.

First of the modern deep-diving research vessels was the bathy-scaph *Trieste*, designed and built in 1953 by Swiss scientist Auguste Piccard and his son, Dr. Jacques Piccard. The vehicle could reach great depths but was not of itself very maneuverable.

The *Trieste*, not commonly referred to as a "submersible" as are other DR/V's, was purchased in 1958 by the U. S. Navy. And in 1960 it took its deepest dive, nearly 7 miles down to the floor of the world ocean.* Jacques Piccard and the Navy's Lieutenant Don Walsh manned the craft for the historic dive, man's deepest into inner space. While there in that dark, mysterious world, one lone fish with eyes and a backbone came within range of the *Trieste's* feeble lights — to the great astonishment of the men inside the craft. This was a discovery of great significance, for until then it was thought that such fish did not inhabit so great a depth.

When the atomic submarine *Thresher* sank off Cape Cod in 1963, *Trieste* joined the search. Later the bathyscaph was rebuilt and the new, more maneuverable craft became *Trieste II*. During 1964 *Trieste II* photographed debris from the lost submarine and brought back identifiable parts from 8,400 feet. It was the tragic loss of the *Thresher* that sparked the upsurge in development of men and machines capable of performing deep-sea search and recovery operations.

---

*Oceanographers refer to the combined seas and oceans of our planet as the *world ocean*. It was in the Pacific's *Challenger Deep* (the Mariana Trench, near Guam) that the *Trieste* descended to 35,800 feet. This is the deepest known spot in the ocean.

Official United States Navy Drawing

TRIESTE II is currently being used to train a nucleus of naval officers and enlisted personnel who will eventually pilot the Navy's new Deep Submergence Rescue Vehicles (DSRVs) and other advanced submersibles. The TRIESTE II is used to develop and improve bottom navigation and underwater search equipment.

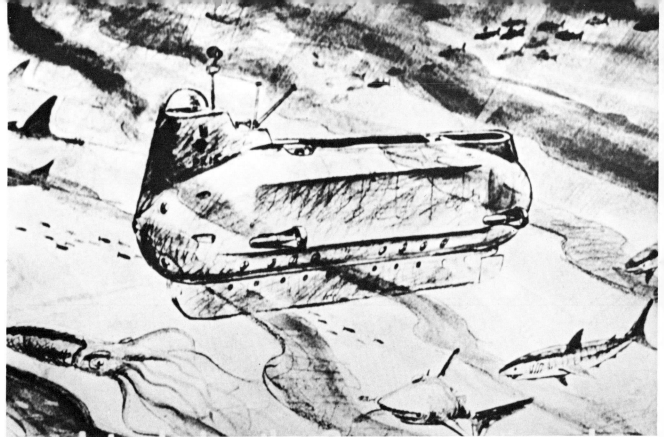

Piccard-Grumman DR/V PX-15.

Grumman Aircraft Engineering Corp.

Another outstanding oceanographic feat will have been accomplished by Dr. Jacques Piccard in the Fall of 1968, if all goes according to plan. It will be a voyage of discovery while drifting north with the Gulf Stream. Starting point will be near Palm Beach, Florida. Waters off Halifax, Nova Scotia, will be journey's end.

The 1500-mile trip will be made in the PX-15, specially designed for the Drift Mission. This venture off the Atlantic coast, submerged in the vast, warm, river-like underseas current, will be a silent journey without motor noise. The PX-15's four 25-horsepower electric motors will be used only to bring the vehicle back into the main flow should it drift into side currents. At most, the motors will be on but a few minutes a day and sea life will not be disturbed by sounds from the monster in their midst.

50

This great floating laboratory can hover motionless and noiseless at any depth down to its limit of 2,000 feet. In it six men will spend four to six weeks at depths ranging between about 300 feet down to 2,000. Anticipated average drift speed is about 1½ knots.

Water temperature, salinity, and ocean currents will be studied. Experiments pertaining to the floating plankton shield, called the Deep Scattering Layer, will be made. This mysterious shield has played havoc with echo sounders and sonar equipment, to the frustration of marine scientists and engineers. Through information such as will be brought back by Dr. Piccard and his crew, it is hoped that problems caused by the Layer can be attacked and remedied. It is hoped that much will be learned about underwater acoustics, resulting in development of better navigational aids and sonar devices for surface ships.

Grumman Aircraft Engineering Corp.

Grumman engineer studies the characteristics of scale model of Piccard-Grumman DR/V PX-15 in test tank.

Model of PX-15.

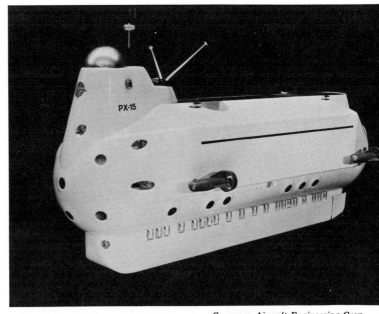

Grumman Aircraft Engineering Corp.

Twenty-nine viewing ports will allow first-hand observation of sea life in the Stream. Everything that comes in view will be watched, from plankton, the bottom of the fish-food chain, to, hopefully, the elusive giant squid.

Sounds in the so-called "silent sea" will be recorded. The chirping of shrimp, the barking of dolphins, and even the sound of water as it moves over the sandy bottom, will be taped.

Pictures taken with still, TV, and motion picture cameras will bring back undersea sights.

Communication with the topside world will be through an ultrasonic telephone link with the sub's mother ship. The ship will make the surface journey directly above the PX-15.

The National Aeronautics and Space Administration (NASA) sees similarities between Dr. Piccard's planned submarine trip and a long-duration voyage into outer space. NASA is interested because the group of scientists in the PX-15 must stay alive and work together for a long time, just as they would on a trip to Mars. The space agency will be watching closely to see how six men get along while eating reconstituted freeze-dried food, rationed water supplies, and in the close confinement of a free-drifting vehicle.

Grumman Aircraft Engineering Corp.

GSV-1, Grumman's second generation work vehicle.

A utility version of the PX-15, the Grumman GSV-I, will provide diver lock-out capabilities to a working depth of 600 feet and be fitted with a crane capable of lifting heavy loads.

New machines and equipment are designed to meet special needs. One such piece of equipment, a *sea plow*, was developed as a new method for laying and protecting transatlantic telephone cables. Cables along the sea floor do not always lie undisturbed. They are sometimes dragged by fishing nets and tidal currents, damaged by sea life, rocks, or sunken wreckage. The results of such damage and impairment of communications are far-reaching. When service is disrupted, government agencies, private businesses, or private individuals may be seriously affected by communication delays. *Operation Sea Plow* was undertaken in an attempt to bury certain portions of the cables beneath the sea floor and thus avoid damage and keep international service intact.

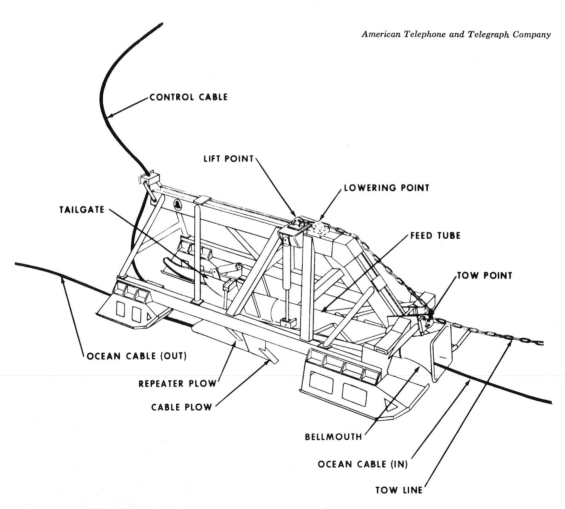

American Telephone and Telegraph Company

CONTROL CABLE

LIFT POINT

LOWERING POINT

TAILGATE

FEED TUBE

TOW POINT

OCEAN CABLE (OUT)

REPEATER PLOW

CABLE PLOW

BELLMOUTH

OCEAN CABLE (IN)

TOW LINE

Diagram of SEA PLOW, developed by Bell Telephone laboratories for American Telephone and Telegraph Company.

American Telephone and Telegraph Company

SEA PLOW is suspended from a crane on the John Cabot, *a Canadian cable repair ship and ice breaker.*

A DR/V made a preliminary survey of the underseas terrain to be followed and came back with an exciting bonus — samples of fossil animal life dating back 15,000 years to the last ice age.

General Dynamics Corp., Electric Boat Division

General Dynamics' miniature submarine STAR III scouted for uncharted rocks and reefs to plot a safe course for the SEA PLOW.

The plow is slowly lowered over the side of the John Cabot. Divers wait below in a motor boat.

As SEA PLOW hits the water a diver hops aboard to straighten out the guy wires from the ship to the plow.

Not only the little underseas work boat and the sea plow itself, but divers and a surface ship were used in the highly successful project. The plow, towed at depths of 120 to 900 feet, moves along on sled-like runners. It plows up the sea floor, paying out and burying cable in the resulting furrows as it goes.

Deep-sea divers adjust a tow line on SEA PLOW.

In its first operation, starting about 35 miles off the New Jersey coast, a 40-mile section of cable to France was buried. Then a 60-mile section of cable to England was plowed under. *Operation Sea Plow* is just one more exciting example of the way skilled men and unique equipment ferret out trouble spots and carry out needed work at the bottom of the sea.

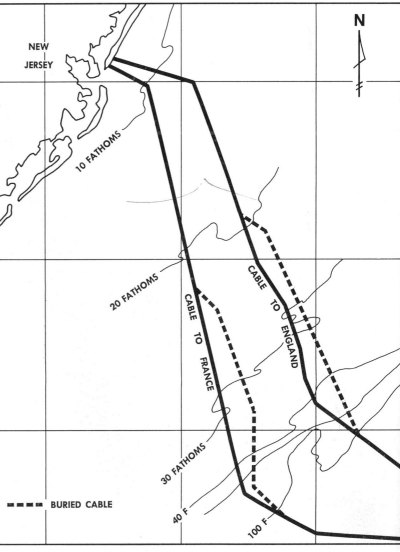

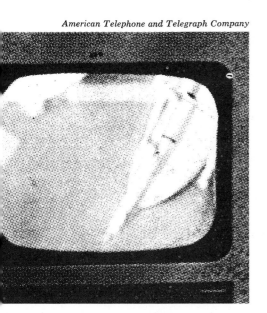

TV views of the plow at work were taken by three cameras on the plow and viewed topside in the ship's control room.

57

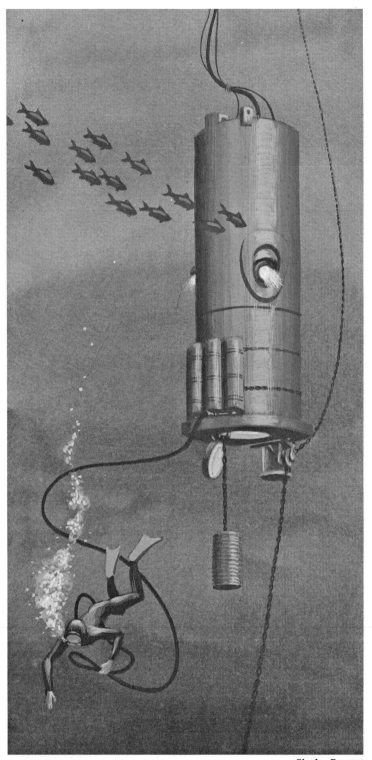

Not only do we have vehicles capable of going down to the bottom of the sea, but man himself has been put down on the sea floor to stay for days at a time.

The dream that man could live and work beneath the sea has held fascination for many people. But three outstanding men in particular, Captain George F. Bond (MC) USN, Captain Cousteau, and Edwin A. Link, have pioneered the way and turned the dream into reality.

Mr. Link, retired industrialist, inventor of aviation's Link Trainer, and expert diver, designed a unique diving cylinder called a Submersible Decompression Chamber (SDC).

The SDC was actually an "elevator" which could carry a diver from ship to the sea floor and up again, being attached to a cable operated by a winch on the mother ship. Its purpose was to serve as living quarters while submerged and as a decompression chamber upon return to shipboard. Air hoses, telephone and power cables connected to the mother ship supplied life support and communication facilities.

Charles Payzant

LINK SUBMERSIBLE DECOMPRESSION CHAMBER

A successful dive lasting more than 24 hours at 200 feet was carried out in early September, 1962. Diver Robert Stenuit, who made the dive, left the cylinder to make brief excursions into the Mediterranean Sea. This was the first Man-In-The-Sea experiment. Previous to this, Mr. Link himself had made a 12-hour test of the cylinder but did not emerge from it into the sea. While submerged, food and newspapers were delivered to him in a watertight jar by his son, also an expert diver.

Captain Cousteau, too, pioneered undersea living later in that same month, with two men who lived and worked for a week 33 feet down in the Mediterranean. The men were housed in the Cousteau-designed habitat, *Conshelf I* (for Continental Shelf).

The habitat was a 17 x 8 foot chamber anchored to the sea floor. The two occupants emerged daily to carry out many pre-planned tasks to test man's ability to perform physical labor under water. At times dives were made to a depth of 85 feet. Food was delivered daily in sealed pressure cookers by divers who had merely to thrust the container up through the ever-open hatch in the floor. Air pressure inside the habitat matched that of the surrounding sea and so kept the water from rising through the hatch.

Captain Bond had long conceived of the possibility of underwater living. An expert diver as well as medical man, it was he who pioneered the concept of *saturation diving* with a naval research project called *Genesis I*.

Working time possible in hard-hat or free-(scuba) diving is short, little can be accomplished before the diver must return to the surface. Depending upon diving depth, decompression time is long.* Without proper decompression, the diver suffers from the painful, and sometimes fatal, condition known as "bends." Goal of the saturation diving concept was to keep man on the bottom for long periods of time so that he could perform useful work.

---

*A diver spending 30 minutes at a depth of 380 feet would require more than 3 hours of decompression before safe return to surface atmosphere. One minute at 600 feet could necessitate more than 12 hours.

If divers were to stay on the bottom, it would be necessary to provide them with a pressurized habitat on the sea floor, a dwelling in which they could live while saturated with a mixture of breathing gases. Then, with the habitat as home base, divers could go out into the surrounding sea to work. Thus an underseas house became part of the saturation diving concept.

Complete saturation of body tissues takes about 24 hours. After that, decompression time is the same for whatever length of time a diver stays below. Decompression of the saturated diver is necessary only once, and that upon return to the surface world after days or weeks of useful work in the sea.

The Cousteau and Link experiments made use of this concept with information gained from *Genesis I* research. And from it was born the United States Navy's Sealab Project as part of the Man-In-The-Sea program.

Under the direction of Captain Bond, SEALAB I, a 40 x 10 foot steel chamber, was home for four men in July, 1964. It was moored 193 feet below the surface, 26 miles off the coast of Bermuda, British West Indies. An umbilical cord of hoses and cables connected *Sealab* with the support barge, or mother ship.

During all hours of the day and night the aquanauts made long excursion dives outside the habitat. They made scientific observations, gathered marine samples, photographed fish and sea floor formations, and performed other useful work. After eleven days on the bottom, they were brought to the surface to undergo decompression. The mission was successful proof of Captain Bond's saturation diving concept. It was proof that man could stay for days beneath the sea and accomplish some useful work while there.

These three experimental habitats — the Link SDC, CONSHELF I, and SEALAB I, were the first cautious steps towards man's becoming a dweller on the ocean floor.

There is friendly competition between Captain Bond, Captain Cousteau, and Mr. Link, but there is also cooperation and sharing of information in an effort to speed up underseas development.

Although Mr. Link and Captain Cousteau were able to put men into the sea to live at an earlier date than was possible for Captain Bond through the Navy with SEALAB I, that mission was the most comprehensive. Scientific data as to how men reacted to underseas life, both mentally and physically, was carefully logged and evaluated in greatest detail for the first time.

The pioneering habitats conducted under the watchful eyes of these three men were only the first of a continuing series. Captain Cousteau and his *oceanauts*, as he calls his crew of expert divers, have established human colonies on the sea floor with CONSHELF II and CONSHELF III.

SEALAB I

Charles Payzant

CONSHELF II

Charles Payzant

In 1963 CONSHELF II housed five men for a month at a depth of 36 feet in the Red Sea. CONSHELF II consisted of a four-armed structure on adjustable legs called "Starfish House." Nearby was an undersea "garage," also on stilts, which housed the Diving Saucer *Soucoupe* for servicing. A third cabin at a 90-foot depth housed two men for a week. These two men worked down as far as 165 feet. Closed-circuit TV constantly monitored the activities both below in the cabin and on the sea floor.

CONSHELF III was even more ambitious. A sphere was lowered 175 feet in the Mediterranean Sea where it stayed for three weeks in 1965. The six men in it performed many tasks on the sea floor, including setting up an oil well-head 150 feet lower down the sloping bottom. The lights of the Diving Saucer helped to illuminate the dark chilly water where the men were working.

At about the same time, but 6,000 miles away, off the coast of La Jolla, California, SEALAB II, the U.S. Navy's second undersea habitat, was submerged at a depth of 205 feet.* This Sealab stayed down for 45 days. Three teams of ten men lived underwater for 15 days each. Scott Carpenter, astronaut-turned-aquanaut, stayed down for 30 consecutive days.

The expert divers on the various teams included medical officers, scientists, photographers, oceanographers, and construction men. Many instruments and much scientific equipment, as well as food and personal gear, had to be fitted into the habitat so space in the underseas home was limited.

*See *Project Sealab,* by Terry Shannon and Charles Payzant, Golden Gate Junior Books, 1966.

SEALAB II

Charles Payzant

Personnel Transfer Capsule (PTC)

But the aquanauts found it a pleasant haven after periods of fatiguing work in the chill waters outside. They found time for fun and relaxation, putting on a concert now and then in funny "Donald Duck" voices caused by the breathing gases they had inhaled.

Divers entered or left Sealab through an always open hatch in the floor. As with the other habitats pressure inside matched that of water outside, thus keeping the sea from coming in. Occasionally, curious fish would swim up and peer through the hatch at the strange visitors to their world. When their 15-day tour of duty below was over the divers returned to the mother ship in a Personnel Transfer Capsule (PTC). From it they entered a Deck Decompression Chamber (DDC) with pressure that of their habitat. This was slowly reduced to that of the surface (requiring about 33 hours). Decompression over, free of the breathing mixture with which they had been saturated, the men could now safely step out into the everyday world of topside and breathe surface air.

64

A deeper undersea stay, but for a shorter period of time, had been made in June, 1964, sponsored by Mr. Link. Again Robert Stenuit went down, this time accompanied by Jon Lindbergh. The two men carried out a successful trial of the Link Submersible Portable Inflatable Dwelling (SPID). This rubber deep-water tent, when inflated with a breathing gas mixture piped down from the ship above, served as living quarters for the divers. A Link SDC took the divers to their temporary home 492 feet down in waters off the Bahamas and returned them to the surface 49 hours later.

The Link IGLOO is an inflatable rubber chamber which, anchored to the bottom, acts as a dry work area for making repairs to underwater installations. Workers return to the nearby SPID for meals and sleep.

SPID and IGLOO

Charles Payzant

Drawing of SEALAB III support vessel and SEALAB III habitat.

Medical van built by Northrop Nortronics for placement aboard SEALAB III support ship. This medical monitoring station will be used to keep check on and for physical examinations of the aquanauts before, during and after their underseas stay.

The Navy's SEALAB III, again with Captain Bond as Principal Investigator, is the most ambitious attempt at undersea living yet undertaken. It will place teams of eight aquanauts down 600 feet to live and work for periods of 12 days each. Plans now call for a Fall 1968 starting date. To imagine a 600-foot depth, think of descending from the top of a 60-story building to the bottom.

Ocean Systems Inc.'s DEEP DIVER

Underseas taxis or shuttle-buses for carrying working divers to and from work stations are more than a science-fiction dream. They, with other devices designed to assist in man's safe entry into and return from the world of inner space, are in various stages of operation and testing.

Deep Diver is the first of today's submersibles from which divers can exit directly onto the sea floor to their work after having been taxied down from the top. Pilot and observer travel in one compartment, two divers in another. As are underseas habitats, the divers' chamber is pressurized to match pressure of the surrounding sea. This keeps water out when the floor hatch is opened and the men go to their sea-floor tasks. Work completed, divers re-enter their chamber, close the hatch, and are taken to another work site or to the surface. Decompression is begun as the men are taken to the top quickly and safely.

DEEP DIVER is lowered into the water from Sea Diver, a specially rigged oceanography vessel owned by Edwin A. Link, of Ocean Systems Inc., who helped design DEEP DIVER.

Ocean Systems, Inc.

Cachalot (the French name for the deep-diving sperm whale) is a complete diving system utilizing the saturation diving concept. A DDC, mounted on a surface barge, and an SDC form the system's key unit. Divers descend to their ocean-floor jobs and return to the surface in the SDC. *Cachalot* allows divers to work at depths to 600 feet for a week or more without paying the penalty of time-consuming decompression each day. Working in shifts, divers return to the surface in the SDC. From it they enter the DDC which serves as a temporary habitat, all the while under the same pressure as that in the sea at the depth where they are working. After meals and rest they return to the sea floor again. The job over, the men then undergo decompression in the DDC.

Divers may work at such varied tasks as testing newly designed tools, making surveys for underseas pleasure parks, constructing permanent ocean-bottom work stations, or building advanced underwater atomic power generating systems.

Westinghouse Underseas Division's CACHALOT is lowered into the water. Note Deck Decompression Chamber on ship.

Westinghouse Electric Corp. Underseas Division

CACHALOT *Submersible Diving Chamber*

CACHALOT *and Deck De- compression Chamber*

Official United States Navy Drawing

The mind must don seven-league boots to keep up with the great underseas engineering projects now underway. The Navy's Large Object Salvage System (LOSS) and its Deep Submergence Rescue Vehicle (DSRV) are two such projects.

The purpose of LOSS is, of course, to recover immense objects from the sea. Plucking such bulky and heavy things as a Navy submarine hull from the sea floor calls for many and varied devices. Pontoons will be attached to the object and foam injected into it to give buoyancy, winches will provide lifting power. But even before actual raising, tremendous lift force will be required to release such enormous weights from the suction of sea-bed muck which may hold them fast in its grip. A surface shipboard control center will coordinate operations.

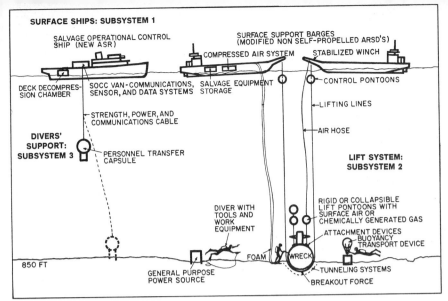

SURFACE SHIPS: SUBSYSTEM 1

SALVAGE OPERATIONAL CONTROL
SHIP (NEW ASR)

SURFACE SUPPORT BARGES
(MODIFIED NON SELF-PROPELLED ARSD'S)

COMPRESSED AIR SYSTEM   STABILIZED WINCH

DECK DECOMPRES-
SION CHAMBER

SOCC VAN-COMMUNICATIONS,
SENSOR, AND DATA SYSTEMS

SALVAGE EQUIPMENT
STORAGE

CONTROL PONTOONS

STRENGTH, POWER, AND
COMMUNICATIONS CABLE

LIFTING LINES

DIVERS'
SUPPORT:
SUBSYSTEM 3

PERSONNEL TRANSFER
CAPSULE

AIR HOSE

LIFT SYSTEM:
SUBSYSTEM 2

DIVER WITH
TOOLS AND
WORK
EQUIPMENT

RIGID OR COLLAPSIBLE
LIFT PONTOONS WITH
SURFACE AIR OR
CHEMICALLY GENERATED GAS

ATTACHMENT DEVICES
BUOYANCY
TRANSPORT DEVICE

850 FT

FOAM   WRECK

GENERAL PURPOSE
POWER SOURCE

TUNNELING SYSTEMS

BREAKOUT FORCE

*U.S. Navy's Large Object
Salvage System*

Official United States Navy Diagram

Planned approach to use of manned submersibles for salvage operations.
Overhead buoyant structure, assembled over wreck, contains a crane which
is operated by manned submersible vehicle above it. A small one-man vehicle
is used to cut away decks and for handling of cargo which is, in turn, loaded
aboard another submarine specially designed for this kind of retrieval.

North American Aviation Inc.

Divers at work.

Divers will do the major work of locating and rigging objects for return to the surface. The men will be equipped with power tools and other devices specially designed for underseas salvage operations. Aquanauts tested many of them during the Sealab experiments.*

Life support for LOSS divers** will be similar to Sealab methods, including a PTC and a DDC. Divers can be lowered to and raised from the work site by the PTC. They can also operate in and out of it, if necessary, while it is on standby on the bottom.

*See *Project Sealab*
**The Navy hopes to have LOSS in operation by 1971 with diver teams working on the bottom at depths to 850 feet.

PTC being developed for LOSS.

Concept of four-man DDC mated to PTC. The outer lock (right) provides a means of entrance for support personnel, a place for medical treatment of divers, and as part of living quarters for saturated divers.

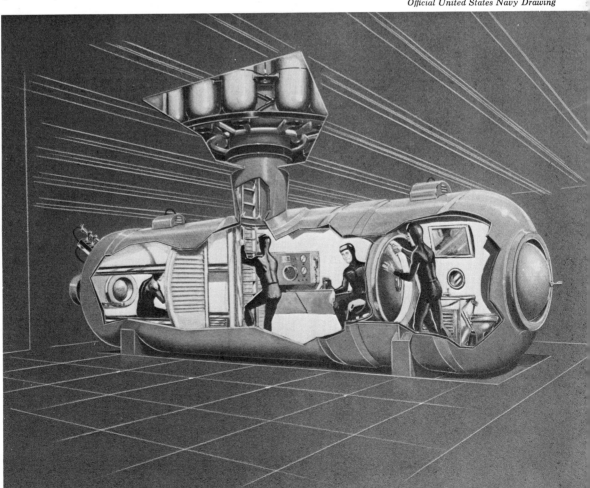

U. S. Navy's Deep Submergence Rescue Vehicle (DSRV)

Official United States Navy Drawing

The purpose of the DSRV is to save lives. Immediately upon receiving notice that a submarine is in distress, land, air and sea units spring into action. Taken from waters of its home port, the DSRV goes by truck to a waiting cargo plane which speeds it to a port nearer the stricken submarine. Another quick trip by truck and the rescue vehicle is put aboard a waiting mother ship to be taken piggyback to its underseas working location.

Then, detached from the mother ship, the DSRV will submerge. It will home in on the disabled submarine with the aid of sonar and high-intensity lights. If there is debris around the sub's escape hatch, the DSRV's mechanical arm will clear it away before covering it with its own hatch.

After mating of the two vehicles, pressure will be equalized between them. Then hatches will be opened and the trapped men, up to 24 at a time, taken aboard the rescue vehicle. This technique will be repeated until all personnel are rescued, the DSRV acting as an underwater shuttle between the disabled submarine and the mother vessel hovering overhead. This great life-saving craft is designed to operate at depths to 3,500 feet.

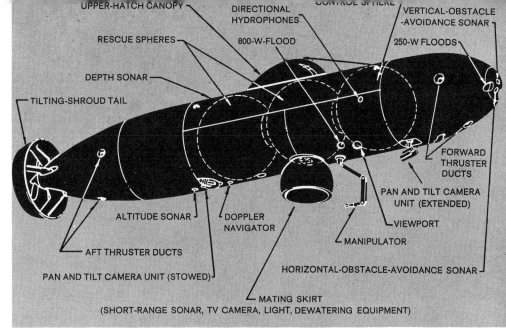

UPPER-HATCH CANOPY · DIRECTIONAL HYDROPHONES · CONTROL SPHERE · VERTICAL-OBSTACLE -AVOIDANCE SONAR

RESCUE SPHERES · 800-W-FLOOD · 250-W FLOODS

DEPTH SONAR

TILTING-SHROUD TAIL

FORWARD THRUSTER DUCTS

PAN AND TILT CAMERA UNIT (EXTENDED)

ALTITUDE SONAR · DOPPLER NAVIGATOR · VIEWPORT

MANIPULATOR

AFT THRUSTER DUCTS

PAN AND TILT CAMERA UNIT (STOWED)

HORIZONTAL-OBSTACLE-AVOIDANCE SONAR

MATING SKIRT
(SHORT-RANGE SONAR, TV CAMERA, LIGHT, DEWATERING EQUIPMENT)

Official United States Navy Diagram

Drawing of DSRV in action

Official United States Navy Drawing

Northrop Nortronics

Drawing by Northrop Nortronics artist shows the various phases, operations and goals of the Navy's Deep Submergence Systems Project.

SUMARINE RESCUE
(1) A deep submergence rescue vehicle is unloaded from a C-141A transport at the scene of a submarine disaster, (2) where it is immediately attached to the "mother" support submarine. (3) The rescue vehicle is then transported "piggyback" to the bottomed submarine, where it is released. (4) Under its own power, it locates and attaches itself to the distressed submarine for transfer of survivors. (5) An enlarged version of the 20,000-foot search vehicle is shown to reveal a mechanical manipulator used to pick up small objects. (6) At a lesser depth, individual escape from a bottomed sub is shown with a minimum of outside assistance.

LARGE OBJECT RECOVERY AND SALVAGE
(7) Inflated salvage pontoons, (8) attached by divers operating from an undersea shelter on the continental shelf, are used to raise a sunken ship. (9) Another method of large object recovery is depicted in the use of cables attached to surface vessels.

DEEP OCEAN OPERATIONS
(10) A deep-diving research vehicle exploring the ocean floor.

MAN-IN-THE-SEA
(11) A "Sealab" station located on the continental shelf.

FUTURE (12) Although not part of the Deep Submergence Systems Project, the artist depicts a futuristic "city in the sea" which will be more feasible as the result of technologies and equipment developed by the program.

North American Aviation, Inc.

Futuristic concept of high-speed, deep-diving attack submarine making a kill.

Concept of underwater missile launcher.

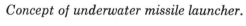

North American Aviation, In

80

North American Aviation, Inc.

Large nuclear-powered underwater detection system. Its surface is covered by sonar transducers used to detect and track enemy subs.

Use of nuclear power beneath the sea for peaceful purposes and for protection of our shores will make it possible for men and machines to stay beneath the surface for very long periods of time. Our atomic-powered submarines have already demonstrated this. Nuclear power will be the key which opens the door to full use of the sea. It will open the way to development of advanced equipment with which man can take from the sea anything it offers and to perform within its depths feats even more remarkable than those now being accomplished.

Underwater Atomic Power Generation System designed by Westinghouse Underseas Division.

Our future in the sea is wide open. We may still have a long way to go before the mighty frontier is completely rolled back. But the start has been made by knowledgeable men of imagination and skill who have turned dreams into action. Men have lived in the sea with success, and advanced underseas work stations and research labs are presently under construction. We have rescue and salvage capabilities that would open the eyes of a Jules Verne. Versatile little work boats accomplish hundreds of tasks beneath the surface of the sea. We have vehicles taking men down to Davy Jones' locker to work, safely returning them to the top again.

And now, so equipped, man is able to carry on his search of the sea whether it be for knowledge or for gold, for sunken ships or for food, or merely for pleasure.

Westinghouse Underseas Division

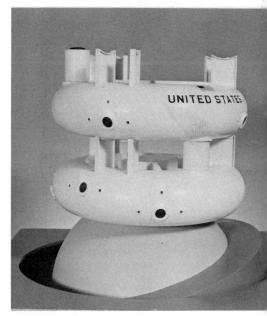

Drawing and model of manned underwater station and research laboratory, designed by Westinghouse for the U. S. Navy. Present plans call for it to be in operation by 1972.

General Dynamics Corp.

Newer subs, such as those under construction at General Dynamics, will
have two manipulators similar to the
human arm. Each has shoulder, elbow
and wrist joints, with an 82-inch reach
when fully extended. When not in use
they can be folded back against the
hull of the submarine. Interchangeable
claw "hands" will enable the subs to
pick up objects as heavy as 100 pounds
— or as delicate as an egg. Detachable
snap-on tools will enable them to cut
cables, drill holes, install or remove
nuts on equipment, and a variety of
other deep-sea construction and repair
work. Clamshell scoops will enable
them to collect mineral and marine
specimens.

Already there is prospecting going on in the sea. Full-fledged diamond mines are operating in gravel beds off the coast of Africa. Oil is being pumped from deep under the sea floor and the search continues for oil deposits from the North Sea to the Gulf of Mexico. Coal is being taken from underseas mines by Japan, and off-shore from Alaska gold is being mined from the sea.

Artist's concept shows North American Aviation's BEAVER MARK IV manned submersible photographing undersea well-head drilling installation. One of the workboat's two divers has exited from the hatch on the underside of the vehicle and is preparing to position the breathing gas cylinder (seen on the ocean floor) in the life support manifold used by the adjacent underwater habitat.

North American Aviation, Inc.

North American Aviation, Inc.

Futuristic concept of use of submarine for fishing, developed by Ocean Systems Operations of North American Aviation Inc.

Farming in the sea has already begun with the cultivation of kelp beds and seaweeds to increase basic materials from which certain foods and drugs are made. *Aquaculture* (farming in the sea) will also include fish farms in days to come. "Bubble curtains" will fence the fish in, trained dolphins will be the "sheep dogs" that herd them. And new, more efficient ways of harvesting fish are coming into being with atomic-powered methods for increasing the catch.

Use of nuclear energy to raise cold, nutrient-laden waters toward surface to attract fish. An Ocean Systems Operations concept.

Artist's conception of Westinghouse Deepstar 20,000

Westinghouse Underseas Division

Tempering daring with a large amount of necessary caution, man is preparing himself to truly become king in that vast region of the deep, the kingdom once reigned over by the legendary King Neptune. The searchers of the sea — man and machine — will continue the investigation of the underseas world until it is as well known as the dry land of our planet.

Pictured on the cover and at right is a concept of a future Ocean Bottom Station by General Electric Co.'s Re-entry Systems Department. It is pictured at a depth of 12,000 feet, but the goal is to emplace and maintain a manned station at depths up to 20,000 feet.

The station is made up of 12-ft. spheres which are joined together by mating 5-ft. hemispheres.

Three glass observation and experiment stations are shown, two manned and two unmanned. Equipped with a variety of sensors, including human, they are in continuous communication with the data center of the habitat. Cutaways show a living compartment and a data center.

The upper portion of the picture shows a ferry vehicle carrying a 12 ft. spherical module as it might be brought down for mating to the habitat.

*Artist's conception of future Westinghouse Underseas
Division underwater vehicle*

And, as Magellan circled the globe in a sailing ship centuries ago, to the astonishment of those of his time, men of the deep sea will one day circle the globe entirely beneath the surface. They will find their way around the Horn, around the Cape of Good Hope, always within viewing distance of the bottom.

Fast underseas cargo ships will take the shortest routes to deliver goods to any place in the world, going under the poles, never coming to the surface between ports.

Perhaps one day some of you will become searchers of the sea. Or you will become aquatic adventurers vacationing in a resort under the sea instead of beside it, or go off on a world cruise in a luxury submersible — thanks to the pioneering work of the sea searchers, the men and machines who have gone to the bottom of the sea before you.

90

A LOOK INTO THE FUTURE.

Charles Payzant

INDEX

Aluminaut, 28, 31; *ill.*, 10, 20, 45
Alvin, 28, 31, 32; *ill.*, 29, 30
aquaculture, 86
aquanauts, 28, 60, 63, 67
Asherah, *ill.*, 47
attack submarine, *ill.*, 80
Autec I, *ill.*, 18

Beaver Mark IV, *ill.*, 85
bends, 59
Bond, Capt. George F., 58, 59, 60, 61, 67

Cachalot, 70; *ill.*, 70, 71
Carpenter, Scott, 63
coal mining, 85
Conshelf I, 59
Conshelf II, 61; *ill.*, 62
Conshelf III, 62
Cousteau, Capt. Jacques-Yves, 15, 58, 59, 60, 61
Cubmarine, 28; *ill.*, 19
CURV, 24, 26, 32, 33; *ill.*, 26, 27, 31, 32, 33, 35

Deck Decompression Chamber (DDC), 64, 70, 74; *ill.*, 70, 75
decompression, 59, 60, 64
Deep Diver, 69; *ill.*, 68, 69
Deep Jeep, 28; *ill.*, 22, 44
Deep Quest, 40, 43; *ill.*, 40, 41, 42
Deep Research Vehicle (DR/V), 14, 79
Deep Scattering Layer, 51
Deep Star 2,000, *ill.*, 23
Deep Star 4,000, *ill.*, 16, 17
Deep Star 20,000, *ill.*, 88
Deep Submergence Rescue Vehicle (DSRV), 72, 76; *ill.*, 76, 77
Deep Submergence Systems Project (DSSP), *ill.*, 78
diamond mining, 85
divers, 13, 59, 63; *ill.*, 13, 74
Diving Saucer (Cousteau), 15, 38, 62; *ill.*, 15
DOWB, *ill.*, 12
Drift Mission, 50

fish farming, 86; *ill.*, 86, 87
future, (a look into), *ill.*, 91

Genesis I, 59, 60
gold mining, 85
GSV-I, *ill.*, 53
Guest, Rear Admiral Wm. S., 28

hydrogen bomb, 28, 35, 37

IGLOO, 65; *ill.*, 65

Large Object Salvage System (LOSS), 72, 74; *ill.*, 73, 79
Lindbergh, Jon, 28, 65
Link, Edwin A., 58, 59, 60, 61, 65, 69

Man-in-the-Sea Program, 60
manipulator "arms," *ill.*, 84

McCamis, Marvin J., 30
medical van, *ill.*, 67
Minard, Glenn, *ill.*, 41
missile launcher, *ill.*, 80
Mizar, U.S. Naval research ship, 31

NASA, 52
Nuclear power, 81

Ocean Bottom Station, *ill.*, 89
oil drilling, 85
Operation Broken Arrow, 28
Operation Sea Plow, 54, 57

Personnel Transfer Capsule (PTC), 64, 74; *ill.*, 64, 75
Petrel, USS, ill., 35
Piccard, Auguste, 48
Piccard, Jacques, 48, 50, 51
Pisces, 38, 39; *ill.*, 38, 39
PX-15, 50, 52; *ill.*, 50, 51

rescue, *ill.*, 79

salvage, *ill.*, 73, 79
saturation diving, 59, 60, 70
Sea Diver, ill., 69
Sealab I, 60, 61; *ill.*, 61
Sealab II, 63; *ill.*, 63
Sealab III, 67; *ill.*, 66, 67
Sealab Project, 60
Sea Plow, 54, 56, 57; *ill.*, 54, 55, 56, 57
Shannon, Terry, *ill.*, 39
Shumaker, Larry, *ill.*, 41
Soucoupe (The Saucer), 15, 38, 62; *ill.*, 15
SORD, 24; *ill.*, 24, 25
SPID, 65; *ill.*, 65
Star II, *ill.*, 14
Star III, *ill.*, 55
Stenuit, Robert, 59, 65
Submaray, ill., 47
Submersible Decompression Chamber (SDC), 58, 65, 70; *ill.*, 58
Swimmer Sled, ill., 46

Thomson, Mack, *ill.*, 39
Thresher, 48
TransQuest, 40
Trieste I, 48
Trieste II, 48; *ill.*, 49

Underwater Atomic Power Generation System, *ill.*, 82
Underwater Detection System, *ill.*, 81
underwater manned station and research lab., *ill.*, 83
underwater vehicle (future), *ill.*, 90

Walsh, Lt. Don, 48
Wilson, Valentine P., 30

94

As an author-illustrator team Terry Shannon and Charles Payzant have produced almost forty books which have delighted a wide audience of young readers. They have covered an amazing variety of subjects and have researched their material in such widely separated locales as Alaska and Paris. Their interest in the subject of "inner space" was sparked by a meeting with Captain Jacques-Yves Cousteau, inventor of the famous Cousteau Diving Saucer, when that submersible (at the time the only craft of its kind in the world) was making a series of dives off the coast of La Jolla in Southern California. For days they watched the dives and Miss Shannon was allowed actually to enter *La Soucoupe* while the little submersible was cradled aboard its mother ship.

The result of this first-hand experience was the highly successful book, *Saucer In The Sea*, written by Miss Shannon and published by Golden Gate in 1965. Then followed *Project Sealab, The Story of the United States Navy's Man-In-The-Sea Program*, this time by both Miss Shannon and Mr. Payzant, who were present at the scene from the very beginning of the Navy's Sealab II experiment and who followed its course day by day by means of the monitor at Topside Control Center while the deep-submergence capsule lay at the bottom of the sea off La Jolla.

Terry Shannon was born in Bellingham, Washington, but has lived in Southern California for many years. Mr. Payzant, a water colorist of note and formerly a top artist with Walt Disney Productions, was born in Halifax, Nova Scotia.